尊重

Social Emotional and Multicultural Learning |
Non-Fiction Series

Copyright © 2022 by Level Learning, INC. and Washington Yu Ying PCS™
Original and Edited Text Copyright © 2022 by Washington Yu Ying PCS™

All rights reserved. No part of this book in whole or part may be reproduced without written permission from the publisher.

Published by Level Learning, INC.

Content Contributors:
Washington Yu Ying PCS™
Level Learning - Jingyao Qi

Illustrations by: Josh Taira

Leveling classification based on Level Learning standard. For full description, visit www.levellearning.com

ISBN 978-1-64040-078-8
Simplified Chinese Edition

About Level Learning:
Level Learning provides a literacy focused curriculum specifically designed for K-12 Chinese as a Second Language classrooms. Our program offers 20 levels of specific and detailed objectives, leveled texts and passages, mastery-based online assessment, and analytics to enable data-driven instruction. Level Learning reading curriculum for both literature and informational text emphasize grammar and comprehension skills to help teachers develop confident and independent Chinese language readers. The non-fiction series of books are specifically designed to support our informational text course based on multiple national standards. To learn more about our entire offering, visit www.levellearning.com.

About Washington Yu Ying PCS™:
Washington Yu Ying PCS is a Mandarin English dual language immersion International Baccalaureate (IB) World school. Yu Ying's mission is to inspire and prepare young people to create a better world by challenging them to reach their full potential in a nurturing Chinese/English educational environment. Yu Ying's comprehensive IB, dual immersion curriculum equips students with global competencies for success in the real world. As a leader in immersion education, Yu Ying is determined to advance Chinese language programs and global citizenry education by helping other schools create and strengthen their Chinese programs. For more information, email: products@washingtonyuying.org

我们都知道要尊重别人，要互相尊重。

哪些行为是尊重他人的表现呢？

不打断别人说话,等别人说完了,我们再说。

这是尊重他人的一种表现。

按顺序排队，不抢先，不插队。

这是尊重他人的一种表现。

听从父母、老师等长辈的话。

这是尊重长辈的一种表现。

我们要尊重别人的感受。

我们也要尊重别人的东西和空间。

别人的东西要经过对方同意才可以动。

别人的地方也要经过对方同意才可以进去。

你明白什么是尊重了吗?

Glossary

	Pinyin	English Definition
尊重	zūn zhòng	respect
别人	bié rén	others
行为	xíng wéi	behavior
表现	biǎo xiàn	to show
打断	dǎ duàn	to interrupt
一种	yì zhǒng	one kind
顺序	shùn xù	order
排队	pái duì	to line up
抢先	qiǎng xiān	to try to be first
插队	chā duì	to cut in line
父母	fù mǔ	parents
老师	lǎo shī	teacher
等	děng	etc.
长辈	zhǎng bèi	one's elders
感受	gǎn shòu	feeling

	Pinyin	English Definition
空间	kōng jiān	space
同意	tóng yì	to agree
动	dòng	to touch, to move
经过	jīng guò	after
进去	jìn qù	to enter
明白	míng bai	to understand

www.ingramcontent.com/pod-product-compliance
Lightning Source LLC
Chambersburg PA
CBHW041222070526
44584CB00001B/58